Striking Strip Quilts

Striking Strip Quilts

16 Amazing Patterns for 2½"-Strip Lovers

Kate Henderson

Martingale
Create with Confidence

Striking Strip Quilts
16 Amazing Patterns for 2½"-Strip Lovers
© 2016 by Kate Henderson

Martingale®
19021 120th Ave. NE, Ste. 102
Bothell, WA 98011-9511 USA
ShopMartingale.com

Printed in China
21 20 19 18 17 16   8 7 6 5 4 3 2 1

Library of Congress Cataloging-in-Publication Data is
available upon request.

ISBN: 978-1-60468-733-0

Mission Statement

Dedicated to providing quality products
and service to inspire creativity.

Credits

PUBLISHER AND CHIEF VISIONARY OFFICER
Jennifer Erbe Keltner

EDITORIAL DIRECTOR
Karen Costello Soltys

DESIGN DIRECTOR
Paula Schlosser

MANAGING EDITOR
Tina Cook

PHOTOGRAPHER
Brent Kane

ACQUISITIONS EDITOR
Karen M. Burns

PRODUCTION MANAGER
Regina Girard

TECHNICAL EDITOR
Monique Dillard

COVER AND INTERIOR
DESIGNER
Connor Chin

COPY EDITOR
Marcy Heffernan

ILLUSTRATOR
Christine Erikson

Dedication

*For Chris. I couldn't have done this without
your encouragement, love, and support.
Thank you.*

Contents

Introduction

Just when I think I might have run out of ideas for strip quilts, I play around with some scraps, draw on some graph paper, or notice something in nature, and a new one pops into my head. If you look around, you can find inspiration everywhere.

It's lucky, then, that I firmly believe a house can never have too many quilts. We lay them on couches and beds, use them to make playhouses, wrap up in them to read on the veranda, and spread them out for picnic blankets. Those days when I think we may finally have enough quilts, there is always a friend or a new baby to sew for.

All of the quilts in this book start with 2½"-wide strips. You can use a bundle or two of precut strips, cut strips from fabrics in your stash, or root through your scrap bin and use up leftovers. If you need tips for acquiring 2½"-wide strips, see "Collecting 2½"-Wide Strips" on page 69. (I'm pretty sure you picked up this book for a reason though!) You'll find more information about working with strips and general patchwork at the back of this book.

Starting with strips that have already been cut is a big time-saver. But I also use other shortcuts such as chain piecing, quick triangle corners, and fast flying geese. If you're not familiar with these techniques, be sure to take a look at "General Quiltmaking Instructions," starting on page 69. It's not that any of these quilts need to be done in a hurry, but if there's a clever way to do a tricky technique, why not try it out?

Whether you're a beginner or an experienced quilter, a fan of precut strips or you're wanting to use up some scraps, there's something in here for you. So grab some fabric and get started!

~Kate

"Summer Holiday"

Pieced and quilted by Kate Henderson ● **Finished quilt: 62½" x 82½"** ● **Finished block: 18" x 18"**

Summer Holiday

We spend our summer holidays down south in Western Australia, where you can be guaranteed of a few cold and rainy days. This is the perfect quilt for curling up and reading on one of those days.

Materials

Yardage is based on 42"-wide fabric.

Fabric: *Linen Cupboard by Emma Jean Jansen for Ella Blue Fabrics*

40 strips, 2½" x 42", of assorted prints for blocks, cornerstones, and binding

3½ yards of white print for blocks, sashing, and border

5⅓ yards of fabric for backing

75" x 95" piece of batting

Cutting

From *each of 12* assorted-print strips, cut:
  1 rectangle, 2½" x 18½" (12 total)
  1 rectangle, 2½" x 16½" (12 total)
  1 square, 2½" x 2½" (12 total)

From *each of 12* assorted-print strips, cut:
  1 rectangle, 2½" x 14½" (12 total)
  1 rectangle, 2½" x 12½" (12 total)
  1 rectangle, 2½" x 6½" (12 total)
  1 rectangle, 2½" x 4½" (12 total)

From *each of 6* assorted-print strips, cut:
  2 rectangles, 2½" x 10½" (12 total)
  2 rectangles, 2½" x 8½" (12 total)

From the remaining 10 assorted-print strips, cut:
  6 squares, 2½" x 2½"
  A variety of strips 14" to 24" long, enough to total
    325" for binding

From the white print, cut:
  41 strips, 2½" x 42"; crosscut *33 of the strips* into:*
    17 rectangles, 2½" x 18½"
    12 rectangles, 2½" x 16½"
    12 rectangles, 2½" x 14½"
    12 rectangles, 2½" x 12½"
    12 rectangles, 2½" x 10½"
    12 rectangles, 2½" x 8½"
    12 rectangles, 2½" x 6½"
    12 rectangles, 2½" x 4½"
    12 squares, 2½" x 2½"

*Cut longest rectangles first; then cut shorter strips from the remaining fabric.

Making the Blocks

Press all seam allowances toward the print fabrics unless otherwise noted.

1 Sew a print 2½" square to a white 2½" square. Sew a white 2½" x 4½" rectangle to the unit as shown.

2 Sew a print 2½" x 4½" rectangle to the left side of the unit from step 1. Sew a matching-print 2½" x 6½" rectangle to the top of the unit.

3 Sew a white 2½" x 6½" rectangle to the left side of the unit from step 2. Sew a white 2½" x 8½" rectangle to the top of the unit.

4 Sew a print 2½" x 8½" rectangle to the left side of the unit from step 3. Sew a matching-print 2½" x 10½" rectangle to the top of the unit.

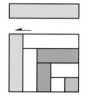

5 Sew a white 2½" x 10½" rectangle to the left side of the unit from step 4. Sew a white 2½" x 12½" rectangle to the top of the unit.

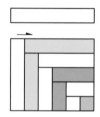
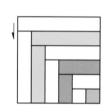

6 Sew a print 2½" x 12½" rectangle to the left side of the unit from step 5. Sew a matching-print 2½" x 14½" rectangle to the top of the unit.

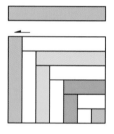
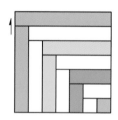

7 Sew a white 2½" x 14½" rectangle to the left side of the unit from step 6. Sew a white 2½" x 16½" rectangle to the top of the unit.

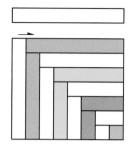
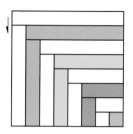

8 Sew a print 2½" x 16½" rectangle to the left side of the unit from step 7. Sew a matching-print 2½" x 18½" rectangle to the top of the unit. The block should measure 18½" square, including the seam allowances. Make 12 blocks.

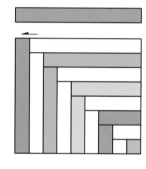
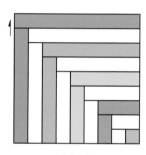

Make 12.

Quilt Assembly

1 Sew three white 2½" x 18½" strips and two print 2½" squares together as shown to make a sashing strip. Press the seam allowances toward the print squares. Make three sashing strips.

Make 3.

2 Arrange the blocks into four rows of three blocks each, rotating the blocks as shown. Sew the blocks together, adding the white 2½" x 18½" strips between the blocks. Press the seam allowances away from the sashing rectangles.

3 Sew the block rows and sashing strips together, alternating them as shown. Press the seam allowances toward the block rows.

4 Sew the eight white 2½" x 42" strips together end to end to make one long strip. From this long strip, cut two strips, 2½" x 78½", and sew them to the sides of the quilt. Press the seam allowances toward the quilt center. Cut two strips, 2½" x 62½", and sew them to the top and bottom of the quilt. Press the seam allowances toward the quilt center.

Finishing the Quilt

1 Layer the quilt top, batting, and backing; baste the layers together. Quilt as desired. I quilted mine with free-motion-quilted starflowers.

2 Referring to "Scrappy Binding" on page 75, join the pieces from the assorted 2½"-wide strips to make a single strip at least 325" long. Use the pieced strip to bind the edges of the quilt. Add a label if desired.

Quilt assembly

"Planets"

Pieced and quilted by Kate Henderson • **Finished quilt:** 40½" x 40½" • **Finished block:** 20" x 20"

Planets

A black-and-cream print background fabric makes bright batiks pop—perfect for a cheerful, modern baby quilt.

Materials

Yardage is based on 42"-wide fabric.

Fabric: *Handcrafted by Alison Glass for Andover and Comma by Zen Chic for Moda Fabrics*

16 strips, 2½" x 42", of assorted bright prints for blocks
1¾ yards of black-and-cream print for background and binding
2⅞ yards of fabric for backing*
49" x 49" piece of batting

*If your fabric is wide enough, you may be able to use a single panel, in which case you need only 1⅜ yards of backing fabric.

Cutting

From *each of 4* bright strips, cut:
  2 rectangles, 2½" x 6½" (8 total)
  2 rectangles, 2½" x 10½" (8 total)
From *each of the remaining 12* bright strips, cut:
  6 squares, 2½" x 2½" (72 total; 4 will be left over)
  2 rectangles, 2½" x 6½" (24 total)
From the black-and-cream print, cut:
  20 strips, 2½" x 42"; crosscut *15 of the strips* into:*
    4 rectangles, 2½" x 16½"
    12 rectangles, 2½" x 10½"
    16 rectangles, 2½" x 8½"
    16 rectangles, 2½" x 6½"
    56 squares, 2½" x 2½"

*Cut the bigger pieces first to make sure you can get all the pieces from 15 strips; otherwise you might need to cut an extra strip.

Making the Blocks

Press all seam allowances open unless otherwise noted. The pieced blocks are assembled by sections A–E, which are then joined to complete four 20" square blocks.

Section A

1 Referring to "Triangle Corners" on page 72, make a triangle corner at each end of bright 2½" x 6½" rectangle with contrasting 2½" squares. Make two matching units.

Make 2.

2 Sew 2½" squares that match the rectangles from step 1 to the sides of a contrasting 2½" square.

3 Sew the units from step 1 to the top and bottom of the unit from step 2.

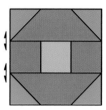

4 Sew matching 2½" x 6½" rectangles that contrast with the rest of the block to the sides of the unit from step 3.

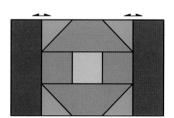

5 Make a triangle corner at each end of a bright 2½" x 10½" rectangle with black-and-cream 2½" squares. The rectangle should match those added in step 4. Make two.

Make 2.

6 Sew the units from step 5 to the top and bottom of the unit from step 4. Make four section A units.

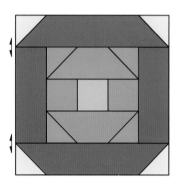

Section A.
Make 4.

Section B

1 Sew a black-and-cream 2½" x 8½" rectangle to a bright 2½" square. Sew a black-and-cream 2½" square and a black-and-cream 2½" x 6½" rectangle to either side of a bright 2½" square.

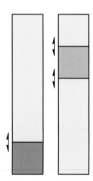

2 Arrange the units from step 1 with two black-and-cream 2½" x 10½" rectangles as shown and sew them together along their long sides. Make four section B units.

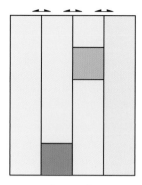

Section B.
Make 4.

Section C

1 Use a black-and-cream 2½" square to make a triangle corner at each end of a bright 2½" x 6½" rectangle. Make two.

Make 2.

2 Sew 2½" squares that match the rectangles from step 1 to opposite sides of a contrasting bright 2½" square.

3 Sew the units from step 1 to the top and bottom of the unit from step 2, as you did for section A.

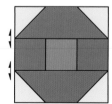

4 Sew a black-and-cream 2½" x 6½" rectangle to the left side of the unit from step 3.

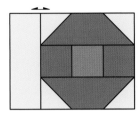

5 Sew black-and-cream 2½" x 8½" rectangles to the top and bottom of the unit from step 4. Make four section C units.

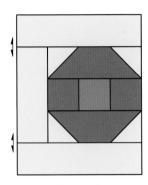

Section C.
Make 4.

Section D

1 Repeat steps 1–3 from "Section C," again using bright rectangles, black-and-cream squares, and bright squares.

2 Sew black-and-cream 2½" x 6½" rectangles to the top and bottom of the unit from step 1.

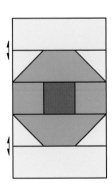

3 Sew a bright 2½" square to one end of a black-and-cream 2½" x 8½" rectangle.

4 Arrange the units from steps 2 and 3 with a black-and-cream 2½" x 10½" rectangle; sew together along their long edges. Make four section D units.

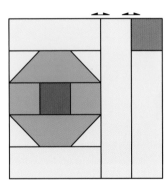

Section D.
Make 4.

Section E

Sew a black-and-cream 2½" square and a black-and-cream 2½" x 16½" rectangle to opposite sides of a bright 2½" square. Make four section E units.

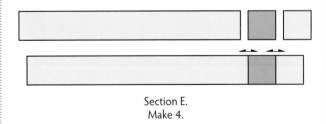

Section E.
Make 4.

Assembling the Block

Arrange sections A, B, C, D, and E as shown below. Sew A to C and B to D, and then sew the two units together. Sew section E to the right side of the unit. Make four blocks.

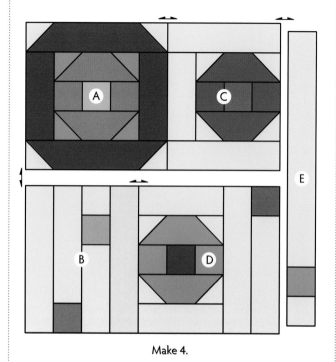

Make 4.

Quilt Assembly

Arrange the blocks in two rows of two blocks each, rotating the blocks as shown. Sew the blocks together in rows, pressing the seam allowances open. Sew the rows together. Press the seam allowances open.

Finishing the Quilt

1 Layer the quilt top, batting, and backing; baste the layers together. Quilt as desired. I free-motion quilted swirly lines with stars.

2 Refer to "Binding the Quilt" on page 75 and use the black-and-cream strips to bind the edges of the quilt. Add a label if desired.

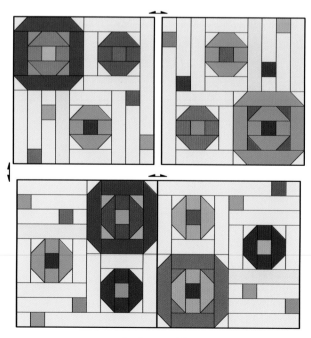

Quilt assembly

Daydream

Ready to do some relaxed sewing? Don't overthink your fabric choices; just grab a stack of fat quarters and get cutting.

Materials

Yardage is based on 42"-wide fabric.

Fabric: *Irome by Kokka Fabrics*

24 fat quarters (18" x 21") of assorted prints for blocks
1⅜ yards of white solid for background and border
⅝ yard of yellow print for binding
4½ yards of fabric for backing
81" x 81" piece of batting
45° ruler at least 8½" tall (such as the large Kaleido-Ruler by Marti Michell) *OR* template plastic

Cutting

From *each of 16* assorted-print fat quarters, cut:
   5 strips, 2½" x 21" (80 total)

From *each of 8* assorted-print fat quarters, cut:
   6 strips, 2½" x 21" (48 total)

From the white solid, cut:
   5 strips, 5½" x 42"; crosscut into 32 squares, 5½" x 5½". Cut the squares in half diagonally to yield 64 triangles.
   7 strips, 2½" x 42"

From the yellow print, cut:
   7 strips, 2½" x 42"

Making the Blocks

1 Organize the 2½" x 21" strips into 32 piles of four strips each. Sew each group of strips together along their long edges. Press the seam allowances in one direction.

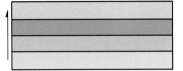

Make 32.

2 Referring to "Templates" on page 70, use the pattern on page 24 to make a 45° triangle template. Align the blunted point with one long raw edge of the fabric and the base of the triangle with the opposite raw edge. Trace along the template's angled edges and cut. Rotate the template 180° and position it next to the angled cut edge, making sure the top and bottom of the triangle align with the fabric edges. Cut a second triangle. Repeat to cut a total of four triangles from each strip set (128 triangles).

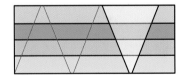

Cut 4 from each strip set; 128 total.

Ruler Instructions

To use the large Kaleido-Ruler, position the blunted tip of the ruler's 45° triangle on one raw edge of the fabric, with the 8½" line on the opposite edge. Cut along the angled edges of the ruler with a rotary cutter.

3 Organize the triangles into 16 groups of eight. If you have four triangles with the seam allowances pressed upward and four triangles with the seam allowances pressed downward in each block, you can alternate them and the seams will nest, making them easier to align and sew together. Sew the triangles

"Daydream"

Pieced and quilted by Kate Henderson • Finished quilt: 68½" x 68½" • Finished block: 16" x 16"

together into pairs and press the seam allowances open. Sew the pairs together to make two half blocks. Press the seam allowances open. Sew the two halves together and press the seam allowances open. Make 16 units.

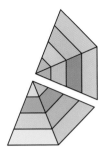 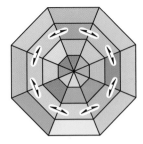

Make 16.

4 Sew a white triangle to each corner of the block. Press the seam allowances open.

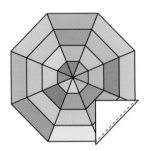 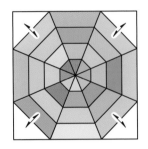

Make 16.

Quilt Assembly

1 Arrange the blocks in four rows of four blocks each. Sew the blocks together into rows and press the seam allowances open.

2 Join the rows. Press the seam allowances open.

3 Sew the seven white 2½" x 42" strips together end to end. Press the seam allowances open. From the pieced strip, cut two side borders, 64½" long, and top and bottom borders, 68½" long.

4 Sew the 64½"-long border strips to the sides of the quilt. Sew the 68½"-long border strips to the top and bottom of the quilt. Press all the seam allowances toward the borders.

Finishing the Quilt

1 Layer the quilt top, batting, and backing; baste the layers together. Quilt as desired. I free-motion quilted an allover scroll pattern.

2 Referring to "Binding" on page 75 and using the yellow-print strips, bind the edges of the quilt. Add a label if desired.

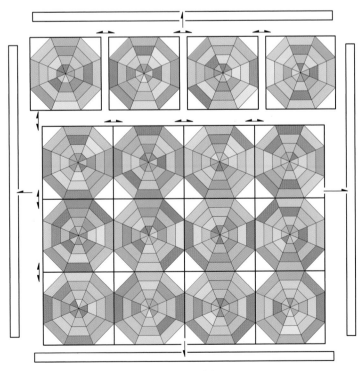

Quilt assembly

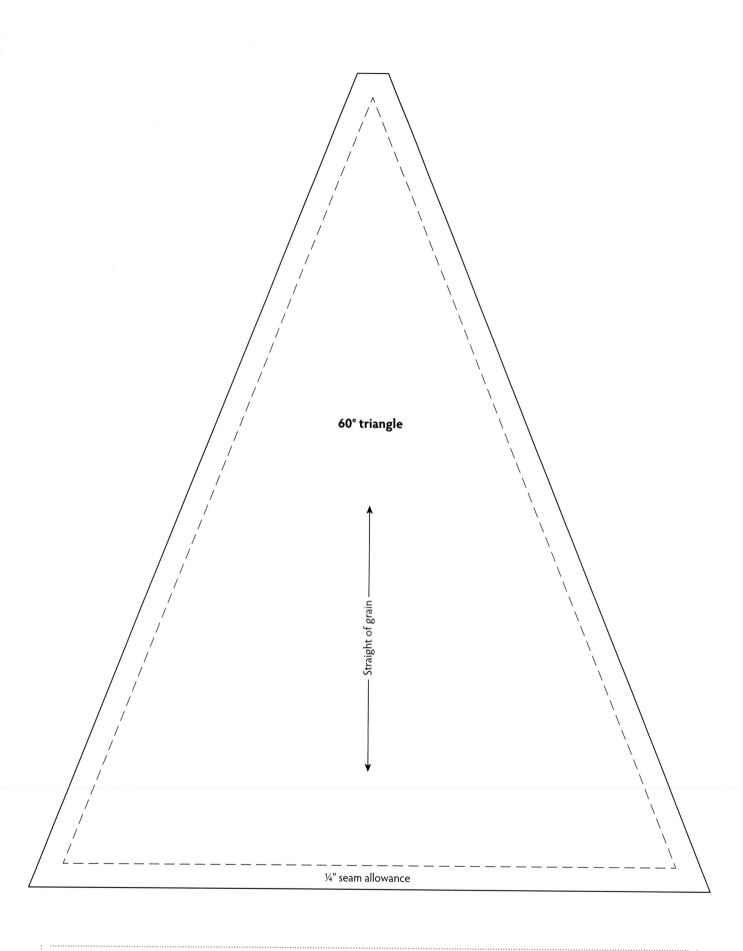

60° triangle

Straight of grain

¼" seam allowance

Vintage Flower Garden

Solid fabrics give this quilt a vintage feel, but you can mix it up with a Jelly Roll of prints and coordinating background solids.

Materials

Yardage is based on 42"-wide fabric.

Fabric: *Bella Solids by Moda Fabrics*

⅜ yard of 6 assorted bright solids in green, red, pink, aqua, orange, and yellow for blocks

4½ yards of navy solid for background, sashing, border, and binding

⅝ yard of white solid for sashing

4⅞ yards of fabric for backing

87" x 87" piece of batting

Cutting

From *each* of the 6 assorted bright solids, cut:

 5 strips, 2½" x 42"; crosscut into:

  12 rectangles, 2½" x 6½" (72 total)

  12 rectangles, 2½" x 4½" (72 total)

  12 squares, 2½" x 2½" (72 total)

From the navy solid, cut:

 59 strips, 2½" x 42"; crosscut *43 of the strips* into:

  20 rectangles, 2½" x 8½"

  40 rectangles, 2½" x 6½"

  144 rectangles, 2½" x 4½"

  205 squares, 2½" x 2½"

From the white solid, cut:

 7 strips, 2½" x 42"; crosscut into:

  100 squares, 2½" x 2½"

Making the Blocks

1 Sew green 2½" x 4½" rectangles to each side of a navy 2½" square. Press the seam allowances toward the navy fabric.

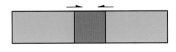

Make 1.

2 Sew navy 2½" squares to each side of a green 2½" x 6½" rectangle. Press the seam allowances toward the navy fabric. Make two.

Make 2.

3 Sew navy 2½" x 4½" rectangles to each side of a green 2½" square. Press the seam allowances toward the navy fabric. Make two.

Make 2.

4 Arrange the units from steps 1, 2, and 3 as shown. Sew them together. Press the seam allowances toward the center of the block. Repeat to make six *each* of green, red, pink, aqua, orange, and yellow blocks with navy backgrounds (36 total).

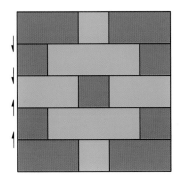

Make 6 of each color for a total of 36.

"Vintage Flower Garden"

Pieced and quilted by Kate Henderson ● Finished quilt: 74½" x 74½" ● Finished block: 10" x 10"

Quilt Assembly

1 Sew a white 2½" square to one end of a navy 2½" x 8½" rectangle. Press the seam allowances toward the navy fabric. Make 10 units.

Make 10.

2 Sew a white 2½" square to each end of a navy 2½" x 6½" rectangle. Press the seam allowances toward the navy fabric. Make 20 units.

Make 20.

3 Join two navy 2½" x 8½" rectangles, four navy 2½" x 6½" rectangles, five navy 2½" squares, and 10 white 2½" squares as shown to make a sashing strip. Press the seam allowances toward the navy fabric. Make five.

Make 5.

4 Lay out the blocks and sashing units from step 1. Piece the top and bottom rows, alternating blocks and units from step 1. Press the seam allowances toward the sashing.

Make 2.

5 Sew the remaining blocks together in rows, alternating blocks and units from step 2. Press the seam allowances toward the sashing. Make four rows.

Make 4.

6 Sew the rows together, alternating rows and long sashing strips from step 3. Press the seam allowances toward the sashing strips.

7 Sew two navy 2½" x 42" border strips together end to end. Press the seam allowances open and cut a 70½"-long strip. Make two. Sew a strip to each side of the quilt. Press the seam allowances toward the border.

8 Sew two navy 2½" x 42" border strips together end to end. Press the seam allowances open and cut a 74½"-long strip. Make two. Sew the strips to the top and bottom of the quilt. Press the seam allowances toward the border.

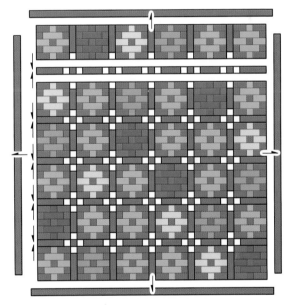

Quilt assembly

Finishing the Quilt

1 Layer the quilt top, batting, and backing; baste the layers together. Quilt as desired. I quilted diagonal straight lines through the center of each block with a walking foot.

2 Referring to "Binding" on page 75 and using the remaining navy strips, bind the edges of the quilt. Add a label if desired.

"Same but Different"

Pieced and quilted by Kate Henderson • Finished quilt: 54½" x 64½" • Finished block: 6" x 8"

The Same but Different

My identical twin girls have always liked to dress similarly to each other and have similar things, but with a slight difference in color or pattern. This quilt pattern is for them; the blocks are nearly the same, but a little bit different.

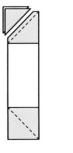

Materials

Yardage is based on 42"-wide fabric.

Fabric: *The Boat House by Sweetwater for Moda Fabrics*

36 strips, 2½" x 42", of assorted prints for blocks
2⅞ yards of white fabric for blocks
⅝ yard of red print for binding
3½ yards of fabric for backing
63" x 73" piece of batting

Cutting

From *each* of the 36 assorted-print strips, cut:
    2 rectangles, 2½" x 8½" (72 total)
    1 rectangle, 2½" x 4½" (36 total)
    6 squares, 2½" x 2½" (216 total)

From the white fabric, cut:
    36 strips, 2½" x 42"; crosscut into:
        72 rectangles, 2½" x 8½"
        36 rectangles, 2½" x 4½"
        216 squares, 2½" x 2½"

From the red print, cut:
    7 strips, 2½" x 42"

Making Block A

1 Referring to "Triangle Corners" on page 72, use white squares to make a triangle corner at each end of a print 2½" x 8½" rectangle. Press the seam allowances toward the print fabric. Make two matching print units.

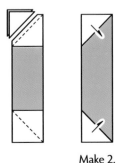

Make 2.

2 Sew a matching print 2½" square to each end of a white 2½" x 4½" rectangle. Press the seam allowances toward the print.

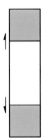

3 Sew the units from step 1 to opposite sides of the unit from step 2, making sure the white corners are on the outside edges of the block. Press the seam allowances outward. Repeat steps 1 and 2 to make 36 of block A.

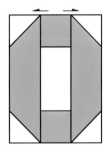

Block A.
Make 36.

Making Block B

1 Use matching print 2½" squares to make a triangle corner at each end of a white 2½" x 8½" rectangle. Press the seam allowances toward the print. Make two units.

Make 2.

2 Sew a white 2½" square to each end of a matching print 2½" x 4½" rectangle. Press the seam allowances toward the print.

3 Sew the units from step 1 to opposite sides of the unit from step 2, making sure the print corners are on the outside edges of the block. Press the seam allowances toward the center of the block. Repeat steps 1 and 2 to make 36 of block B.

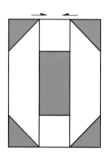

Block B.
Make 36.

Quilt Assembly

Arrange the blocks in eight rows of nine blocks each, alternating blocks A and B. Sew the blocks together into rows, pressing the seam allowances toward block A. Sew the rows together. Press the seam allowances in one direction.

Finishing the Quilt

1 Layer the quilt top, batting, and backing; baste the layers together. Quilt as desired. I quilted straight vertical lines 1" apart.

2 Referring to "Binding" on page 75 and using the red strips, bind the edges of the quilt. Add a label if desired.

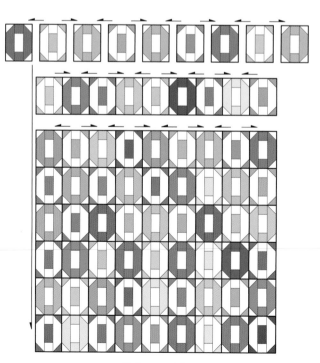

Quilt assembly

Heading Home

I used precut strips to make the flying geese in this quilt, but this pattern is also perfect for using your scraps.

Materials

Yardage is based on 42"-wide fabric.

Fabric: *Gardenvale by Jen Kingwell for Moda Fabrics*

40 strips, 2½" x 42", of assorted prints for blocks and binding

2⅓ yards of white fabric for background

⅝ yard of white-with-black dot for blocks

½ yard of black fabric for blocks

3⅓ yards of fabric for backing

60" x 60" piece of batting

Cutting

From *each of 20* assorted-print strips, cut:*

3 rectangles, 2½" x 4½" (60 total)

From *each of 12* assorted-print strips, cut:*

3 rectangles, 2½" x 4½" (36 total)

1 square, 2½" x 2½" (12 total)

From *each of 8* assorted-print strips, cut:*

4 rectangles, 2½" x 4½" (32 total)

From the white fabric, cut:

24 strips, 2½" x 42"; crosscut into:

16 rectangles, 2½" x 16½"

256 squares, 2½" x 2½"

2 strips, 4⅞" x 42"; crosscut into 12 squares, 4⅞" x 4⅞"

1 strip, 5¼" x 42"; crosscut into 4 squares, 5¼" x 5¼". Cut the squares into quarters diagonally to yield 16 triangles.

From the white-with-black dot, cut:

5 squares, 8½" x 8½"

2 squares, 8⅞" x 8⅞"; cut in half diagonally to yield 4 triangles

1 square, 9¼" x 9¼"; cut into quarters diagonally to yield 4 triangles

From the black fabric, cut:

2 strips, 4⅞" x 42"; crosscut into 12 squares, 4⅞" x 4⅞"

1 strip, 5¼" x 42"; crosscut into 4 squares, 5¼" x 5¼". Cut the squares into quarters diagonally to yield 16 triangles.

*Save remaining strips for binding. See "Scrappy Binding" on page 75.

Planning Ahead

I used a whole Jelly Roll to provide lots of different fabrics for my quilt, but it can be made with just 20 strips. Cut a total of 128 rectangles, 2½" x 4½", and 12 squares, 2½" x 2½". You'll also need ½ yard of fabric for a one-fabric binding.

Making the Blocks

Press all seam allowances open unless otherwise noted.

1 Referring to "Flying-Geese Units" on page 72, use two white 2½" squares and a print 2½" x 4½" rectangle to make a flying-geese unit. Make 128 units.

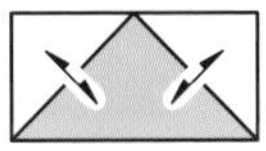

Make 128.

2 Sew four flying-geese units together as shown. Make 32.

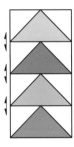

Make 32.

3 Draw a diagonal line across the back of a white 4⅞" square and place it right sides together with a black 4⅞" square. Sew ¼" from each side of the drawn line. Cut the squares apart on the drawn lines to make 24 half-square-triangle units.

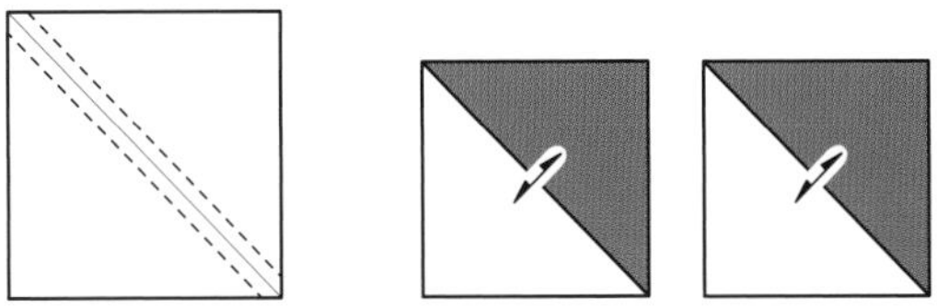

Make 24 total.

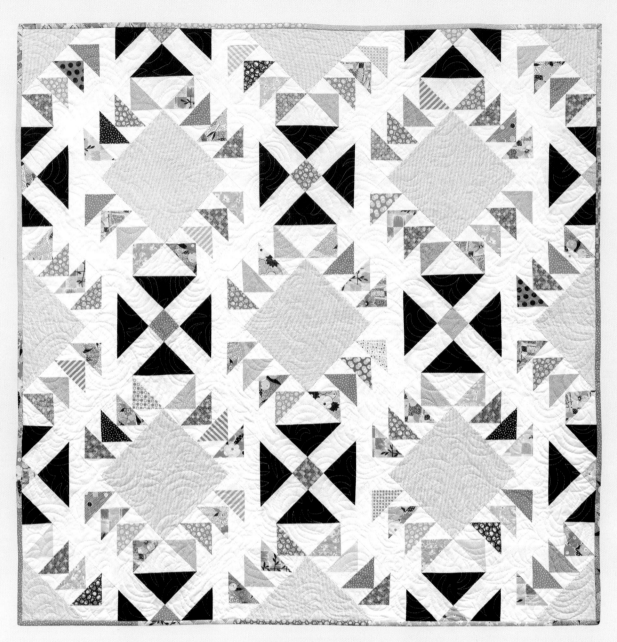

"Heading Home"

Pieced and quilted by Kate Henderson ● Finished quilt: 51½" x 51½" ● Finished block: 16" x 16"

4 Sew a half-square-triangle unit from step 3 to each side of a unit from step 2 as shown, paying attention to the orientation of the flying-geese units. Make 10 units.

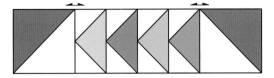

Make 10.

5 Sew a unit from step 2 to each side of a white-with-black dot 8½" square. Make Five.

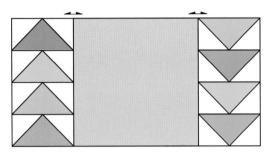

Make 5.

6 Sew units from step 4 to the top and bottom of a unit from step 5 as shown. Make five blocks.

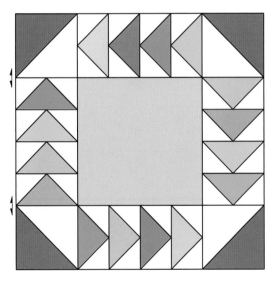

Make 5.

Making the Half Blocks

Press all seam allowances open.

1 Sew a white and a black quarter-square triangle together. Repeat to make a mirror image of the first one. Make eight of each.

Make 8 of each.

2 Sew together a half-square-triangle unit, a four-geese unit, and a quarter-square-triangle unit, making sure the units are oriented as shown.

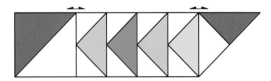

3 Sew a four-geese unit to a white-with-black dot half-square triangle, making sure the pieces are oriented as shown.

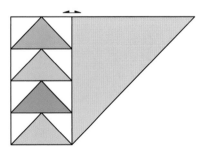

4 Sew the unit from step 2 and another quarter-square triangle to the unit from step 3 as shown. Make four half blocks, two with geese flying toward the half-square-triangle unit and two with the geese flying away.

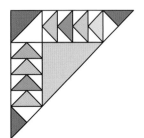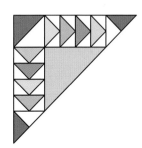

Make 2 of each.

Making the Quarter Blocks

Press all seam allowances open.

1 Sew quarter-square-triangle units to each side of a four-geese unit.

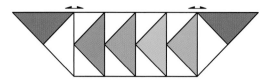

2 Sew a white-with-black dot half-square triangle to the unit from step 1 as shown. Repeat to make four quarter blocks, two with the geese flying in one direction and two with the geese flying in the opposite direction.

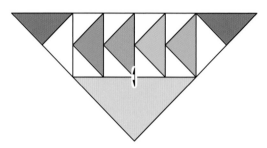

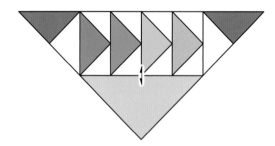

Make 2 of each.

Quilt Assembly

1 Using a ruler and rotary cutter, trim eight of the print 2½" squares ¼" from the diagonal centerline of the square as shown. This is similar to the trimming for triangle corners on page 72. Keep the larger section; the smaller triangle will not be needed.

2 Arrange the blocks, half blocks, quarter blocks, remaining print squares, white 2½" x 16½" rectangles, and trimmed squares from step 1 as shown in the quilt assembly diagram. Sew the pieces together into diagonal rows. Press the seam allowances toward the white rectangles.

3 Sew the rows together. Press the seam allowances toward the white rectangles.

Finishing the Quilt

1 Layer the quilt top, batting, and backing; baste the layers together. Quilt as desired. I free-motion quilted an allover echoing spiky pattern.

2 Referring to "Scrappy Binding" on page 75, join the leftover pieces from the print 2½"-wide strips to make a single strip at least 220" long. Use the strip to bind the edges of the quilt. Add a label if desired.

Quilt assembly

Harvest Time

The colors of the Jelly Roll used for this quilt took me back to my childhood and harvest time on our farm. Make sure you choose contrasting strips for each block to make the pattern pop.

Materials

Yardage is based on 42"-wide fabric.

Fabric: *Persimmon by Basic Grey for Moda Fabrics*

40 strips, 2½" x 42", of assorted prints for blocks
2⅞ yards of white fabric for background
¾ yard of blue print for cornerstones and binding
3¾ yards of fabric for backing
67" x 81" piece of batting

Cutting

From *each* of the 40 assorted-print strips, cut:
   3 rectangles, 2½" x 13½" (120 total)

From the white fabric, cut:
   37 strips, 2½" x 42"; crosscut into:
      320 squares, 2½" x 2½"
      49 rectangles, 2½" x 12½"

From the blue print, cut:
   9 strips, 2½" x 42"; crosscut *2 of the strips* into
      30 squares, 2½" x 2½"

Making the Blocks

Press all seam allowances open.

1 Organize the 2½" x 13½" rectangles into 20 groups. Each group needs three strips *each* of two different fabrics. Sew matching strips to both long sides of a contrasting strip. Cut the strip set into two 6½"-wide segments; the segments should be 6½" square. Repeat with the other three strips to make two segments in the reverse color combination. Make 40 strip sets and cut two segments from each.

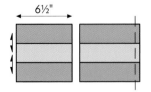 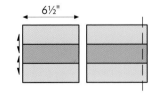

Make 1 strip set from each group.
Cut 2 segments from each strip set.

2 Referring to "Triangle Corners" on page 72, use the white 2½" squares to add a triangle to each corner of the pieced squares. Make 40 of each.

Make 2 from each group, 40 total. Make 2 from each group, 40 total.

3 Arrange four matching units as shown below, rotating alternate units. Sew the units into pairs. Sew the pairs together and press the seam allowances open. Make 20 blocks.

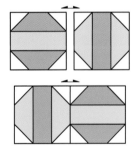 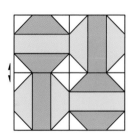

Make 20.

Quilt Assembly

1 Sew five blue 2½" squares and four white 2½" x 12½" rectangles together as shown to make a sashing strip. Press the seam allowances toward the white rectangles. Make six sashing strips.

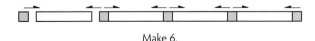

Make 6.

"Harvest Time"

Pieced and quilted by Kate Henderson • **Finished quilt: 58½" x 72½"** • **Finished block: 12" x 12"**

2 Sew four blocks and five white 2½" x 12½" rectangles together, alternating them as shown. Press the seam allowances toward the white rectangles. Make five rows.

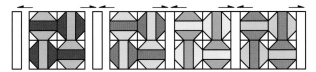

Make 5.

3 Lay out the assembled rows and sashing strips. Sew them together and press the seam allowances toward the sashing strips.

Finishing the Quilt

1 Layer the quilt top, batting, and backing; baste the layers together. Quilt as desired. I free-motion quilted swirls and leaves.

2 Referring to "Binding" on page 75 and using the blue strips, bind the edges of the quilt. Add a label if desired.

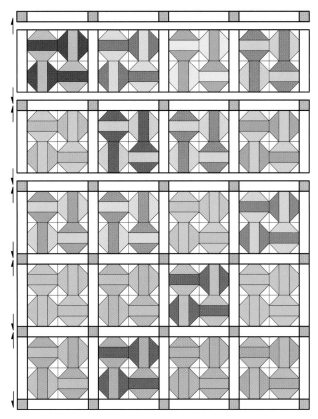

Quilt assembly

"By the Seashore"

Pieced and quilted by Kate Henderson ● Finished quilt: 59½" x 59½" ● Finished block: 12" x 12"

By the Seashore

Each 12" block is composed of nine simple pieced units, making this quilt much easier to assemble than it looks. I chose strong contrasting colors so each part of the block would be easily seen.

Materials

Yardage is based on 42"-wide fabric.

Fabric: *Daysail by Bonnie and Camille for Moda Fabrics*

31 strips, 2½" x 42", of assorted prints for blocks
2⅞ yards of white fabric for background
⅝ yard of green print for binding
3¾ yards of fabric for backing
68" x 68" piece of batting

Cutting

From *each of 26* assorted-print strips, cut:
    4 rectangles, 2½" x 4½" (104 total)
    8 squares, 2½" x 2½" (208 total)

From *each of 5* assorted-print strips, cut:
    16 squares, 2½" x 2½" (80 total; 4 will be left over)

From the white fabric, cut:
    26 strips, 2½" x 42"; crosscut into:
        36 rectangles, 2½" x 12½"
        52 rectangles, 2½" x 4½"
        104 squares, 2½" x 2½"
    1 strip, 18⅛" x 42"; crosscut into 2 squares,
        18⅛" x 18⅛". Cut the squares into quarters
        diagonally to yield 8 triangles.
    1 strip, 9⅜" x 42"; crosscut into 2 squares,
        9⅜" x 9⅜". Cut the squares in half diagonally
        to yield 4 triangles.

From the green print, cut:
    7 strips, 2½" x 42"

Planning Ahead

Before you start sewing, sort the print rectangles and squares into 13 piles, one for each block. This will make it easier to achieve variation within the blocks and will ensure you have enough matching prints when you need them. In each pile gather the following pieces:

- Fabric 1: 4 rectangles, 2½" x 4½", and 4 squares, 2½" x 2½"
- Fabric 2: 4 squares, 2½" x 2½"
- Fabric 3: 8 squares, 2½" x 2½", and 4 rectangles, 2½" x 4½"
- Fabric 4: 2 squares, 2½" x 2½"
- Fabric 5: 2 squares, 2½" x 2½"
- White: 4 rectangles, 2½" x 4½", and 8 squares, 2½" x 2½"

Making the Blocks

Press all seam allowances open.

1 Sew two contrasting print 2½" squares together. Sew a 2½" x 4½" rectangle that matches the second square to the unit as shown. Make four blocks.

Make 4.

2 Referring to "Flying-Geese Units" on page 72, use two white 2½" squares and a print 2½" x 4½" rectangle to make a flying-geese unit. Make four flying-geese units.

Make 4.

3 Use two matching print 2½" squares and a white 2½" x 4½" rectangle to make a flying-geese unit. Make four flying-geese units.

Make 4.

4 Sew a unit from step 2 to a unit from step 3 as shown. Make four blocks.

Make 4.

5 Sew two contrasting print 2½" squares together to make a two-patch unit. Make one more unit. Sew the two units together.

6 Sew the small blocks together as shown to form a big block. Repeat to make 13 blocks.

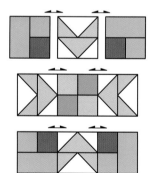 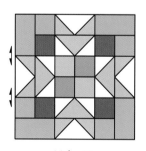

Make 13.

Quilt Assembly

1 Trim 12 of the remaining print squares ¼" from the diagonal centerline of the square as shown. This is similar to the trimming for triangle corners on page 72. Keep the larger section; the smaller triangle will not be needed.

2 Arrange the blocks, white 2½" x 12½" rectangles, setting triangles, remaining print squares, and trimmed squares from step 1 as shown in the quilt assembly diagram. Sew the pieces together into diagonal rows. Press the seam allowances toward the white rectangles.

3 Sew the rows together. Press the seam allowances toward the white rectangles.

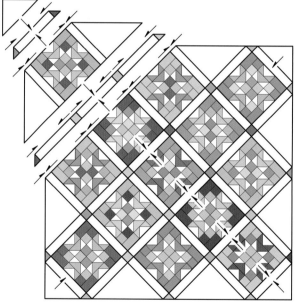

Quilt assembly

Finishing the Quilt

1 Layer the quilt top, batting, and backing; baste the layers together. Quilt as desired. I free-motion quilted an allover wave pattern.

2 Referring to "Binding" on page 75, use the green strips to bind the edges of the quilt. Add a label if desired.

Rainbow Twist

Brightly colored fabrics really pop against a black background. With big blocks and easy piecing, this quilt will be finished in no time.

Materials

Yardage is based on 42"-wide fabric.

Fabric: *From my scrap bucket and Sketch by Timeless Treasures*

6 strips, 2½" x 42" *each*, of assorted prints in pink, blue, green, red, purple, brown, gray, yellow, and orange for blocks

3 yards of black print for background and binding

4¾ yards of fabric for backing

85" x 85" piece of batting

Cutting

From *each* of the assorted-print strips, cut:

4 rectangles, 2½" x 6½" (216 total)

From the black print, cut:

12 strips, 6½" x 42"; crosscut into 36 rectangles, 6½" x 12½"

8 strips, 2½" x 42"

Cutting

The cutting instructions are written for assorted colorful 2½" strips, but I raided my scrap bucket and used as many different print fabrics as I could to give the quilt a scrappy look.

Making the Blocks

1 Sew six pink 2½" x 6½" rectangles together along their long edges. Press the seam allowances in one direction. Make four.

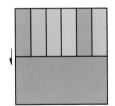

Make 4.

2 Sew a black 6½" x 12½" rectangle to the unit from step 1. Press the seam allowances toward the black fabric. Make four.

Make 4.

3 Arrange the four units from step 2 as shown. Sew the top two together and the bottom two together and press the seam allowances in opposite directions. Sew the top and bottom units together and press the seam allowances in one direction. Repeat to make one block each using blue, green, red, purple, brown, gray, yellow, and orange (nine total).

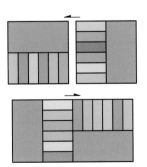
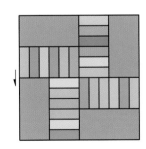

Make 1 of each color for a total of 9.

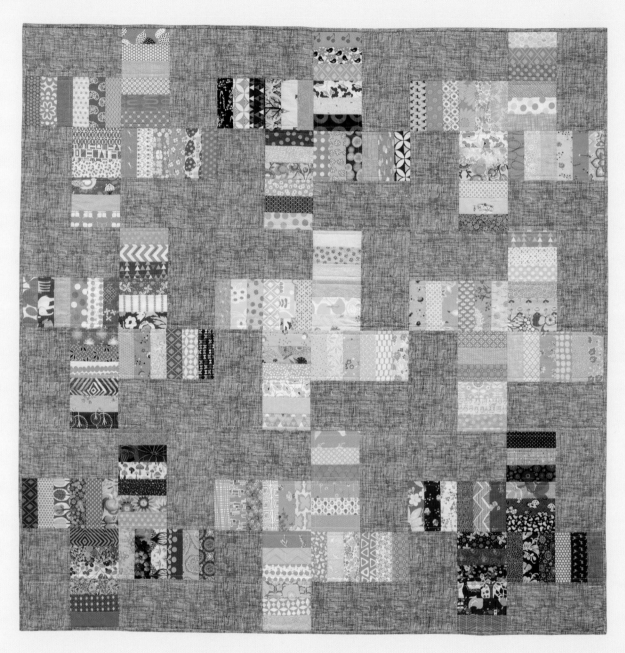

"Rainbow Twist"

Pieced and quilted by Kate Henderson • **Finished quilt:** 72½" x 72½" • **Finished block:** 24" x 24"

Quilt Assembly

Arrange the blocks in three rows of three blocks each. Sew the blocks together in rows, pressing the seam allowances in alternating directions from row to row. Sew the rows together. Press the seam allowances in one direction.

Finishing the Quilt

1 Layer the quilt top, batting, and backing; baste the layers together. Quilt as desired. With a walking foot, I quilted straight lines horizontally and vertically to form a grid.

2 Referring to "Binding" on page 75 and using the black 2½" strips, bind the edges of the quilt. Add a label if desired.

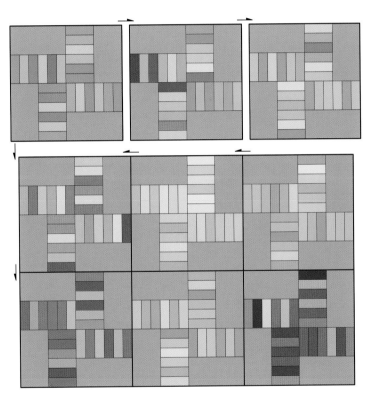

Quilt assembly

"Starburst"

Pieced and quilted by Kate Henderson ● Finished quilt: 42½" x 54½" ● Finished block: 6" x 6"

Starburst

A simple two-block design with plenty of punch and movement makes a perfect gift for a baby or small child.

Materials

Yardage is based on 42"-wide fabric.

Fabric: *Fresh Air by American Jane for Moda Fabrics*

26 strips, 2½" x 42", of assorted prints for blocks and binding

2⅜ yards of cream fabric for background

2⅞ yards of fabric for backing

51" x 63" piece of batting

Cutting

From *each of 12* assorted-print strips, cut:
   8 rectangles, 2½" x 4½" (96 total)

From *each of 8* assorted-print strips, cut:
   4 rectangles, 2½" x 4½" (32 total)

From the remainders of the assorted-print strips and the 6 additional strips, cut:
   63 squares, 2½" x 2½"
   A variety of strips 10" to 20" long, enough to total 215"

From the cream fabric, cut:
   31 strips, 2½" x 42"; crosscut into:
      318 squares, 2½" x 2½"
      62 rectangles, 2½" x 6½"

Making the Star Blocks

1 Referring to "Triangle Corners" on page 72, use a cream 2½" square to make a triangle corner at each end of a print 2½" x 4½" rectangle as shown. Pay attention to the direction you sew the triangle corners; they must be sewn the same way or your star blocks will spin in different directions. Press the seam allowances toward the print. Make four matching units.

Make 4.

2 Sew a contrasting print square to a unit from step 1, sewing a partial seam beginning at the outer edge and sewing about halfway. Press the seam allowances toward the center square.

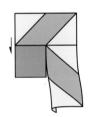

3 Sew the remaining three units from step 1 to the center square counterclockwise as shown. Press the seam allowances toward the center square. After the last unit is attached, finish sewing the partial seam to complete the block. Make 32 blocks total.

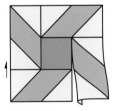 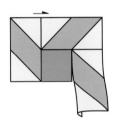

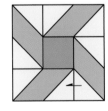

Make 32.

Making the Square Blocks

1 Sew cream 2½" squares to the top and bottom of a print 2½" square. Press the seam allowances toward the print square.

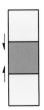

2 Sew cream 2½" x 6½" rectangles to both sides of a unit from step 1. Press the seam allowances toward the center. Make 31 blocks.

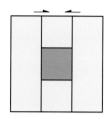

Make 31.

Quilt Assembly

Arrange the blocks in nine rows of seven blocks each, alternating the star and square blocks. Sew the blocks together in rows, pressing the seam allowances toward the square blocks. Sew the rows together. Press the seam allowances in one direction.

Finishing the Quilt

1 Layer the quilt top, batting, and backing; baste the layers together. Quilt as desired. I free-motion quilted loops and swirls.

2 Referring to "Scrappy Binding" on page 75, join the assorted 2½"-wide strips to make a strip at least 215" long. Use the pieced strip to bind the edges of the quilt. Add a label if desired.

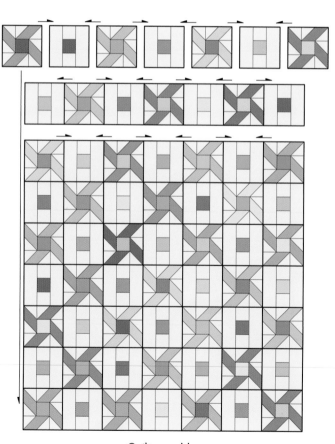

Quilt assembly

Folk-Art Flowers

Inspired by beautiful folk-art flower designs, I originally designed this quilt with solid fabrics, but gradually a few prints crept in. Eventually it became a scrappy quilt using little bits of all my favorite fabrics from my scrap bucket. For something different, try it with aqua flowers and gray leaves.

Materials

Yardage is based on 42"-wide fabric.

Fabric: *From my scrap bucket*

114 squares, 2½" x 2½", of assorted red prints
   for blocks
106 squares, 2½" x 2½", of assorted green prints
   for blocks
4½ yards of white with red dot for large panels
1⅛ yards of white fabric for background
⅔ yard of black-and-white print for binding
4¾ yards of fabric for backing
85" x 85" piece of batting

Cutting the Squares

I wanted to make my flowers and leaves scrappy, but if you prefer to cut the red and green squares from strips, you'll need 8 red strips, 2½" x 42", and 7 green strips, 2½" x 42".

Cutting

From the white with red dot, cut:
   1 rectangle, 34½" x 72½"
   1 rectangle, 16½" x 72½"
From the white fabric, cut:
   1 strip, 4½" x 42"; crosscut into 8 squares,
      4½" x 4½"
   12 strips, 2½" x 42"; crosscut *8 of the strips* into:
      12 rectangles, 2½" x 8½"
      10 rectangles, 2½" x 6½"
      42 squares, 2½" x 2½"
From the black-and-white print, cut:
   8 strips, 2½" x 42"

Making the Flower Blocks

Press all seam allowances open.

1 Referring to "Triangle Corners" on page 72, use a red 2½" square to make a triangle corner at one corner of a white 4½" square. Make eight.

Make 8.

2 Make a four-patch unit by sewing four red 2½" squares together in pairs, and then sewing the two pairs together. Make 16.

Make 16.

3 Referring to "Half-Square-Triangle Units" on page 72, make a half-square-triangle unit using one white and one red 2½" square. Make eight.

Make 8.

"Folk-Art Flowers"

Pieced and quilted by Kate Henderson ● Finished quilt: 72½" x 72½" ● Finished block: 36" x 36"

4 Using a half-square-triangle unit from step 3 and three red 2½" squares, make a four-patch unit by sewing them together in pairs as shown. Sew the two pairs together. Make eight.

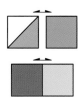

Make 8.

5 Sew a unit from step 4 and a four patch from step 2 together as shown. Sew a unit from step 2 and a unit from step 1 together as shown. Sew the two units together. Make eight.

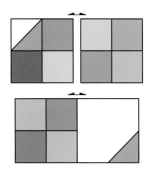 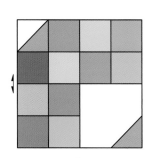

Make 8.

6 Sew a red 2½" square to one end of a white 2½" x 6½" rectangle. Make six.

Make 6.

7 Sew a unit from step 5 to each side of a unit from step 6. Make two.

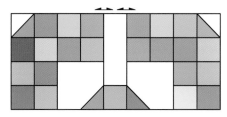

Make 2.

8 Sew a red, white, and two green 2½" squares together as shown. Make two.

Make 2.

9 Sew a unit from step 5 to each side of a unit from step 8. Make two.

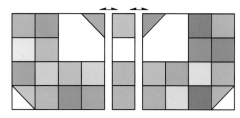

Make 2.

10 Sew units from step 6 to opposite sides of a red 2½" square. Make two.

Make 2.

11 Sew units from steps 7, 9, and 10 together as shown. Make two blocks.

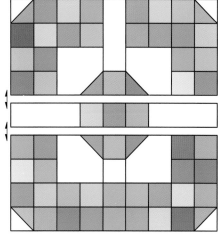

Make 2.

Making the Leaf Blocks

Press all seam allowances open.

1 Referring to "Half-Square-Triangle Units," make a half-square-triangle unit using one white and one green 2½" square. Make 32.

Make 32.

2 Sew half-square-triangle units from step 1 to opposite sides of a green 2½" square. Make eight.

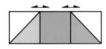

Make 8.

3 Sew three green 2½" squares together. Make four.

Make 4.

4 Sew the units from step 2 to the top and bottom of the unit from step 3. Make four.

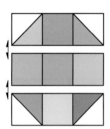

Make 4.

5 Sew a white 2½" x 6½" rectangle to one side of the unit from step 4. Make four.

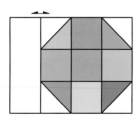

Make 4.

6 Sew two half-square-triangle units from step 1 and two green 2½" squares together. Make eight.

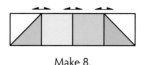

Make 8.

7 Sew four green 2½" squares together. Make four.

Make 4.

8 Join the units from step 6 to the top and bottom of the units from step 7. Make four.

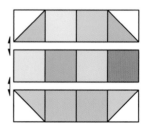

Make 4.

9 Sew together a unit from step 5, a unit from step 8, and three white 2½" x 8½" rectangles as shown. Make two and two with the small leaf reversed.

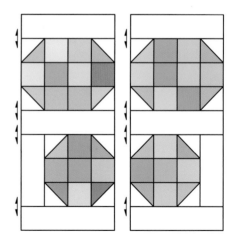

Make 2 of each.

10 Sew together nine green 2½" squares in a column. Sew a leaf unit and a reverse leaf unit from step 9 to each side of the green square unit. Make two blocks.

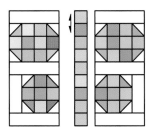 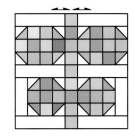

Make 2.

Quilt Assembly

Press all seam allowances open.

1 Sew the flower and leaf blocks together.

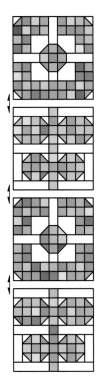

2 Sew two of the white 2½" x 42" strips together end to end and cut a strip 72½" long; make two. Sew a strip to each side of the flower and leaf blocks.

3 Sew the white-with-red-dot 16½" x 72½" rectangle to the left side of the quilt, and then sew the 34½" x 72½" rectangle to the right side.

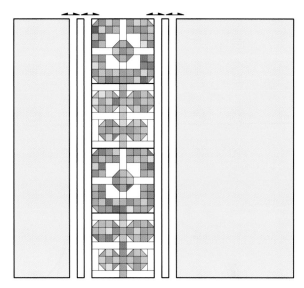

Quilt assembly

Finishing the Quilt

1 Layer the quilt top, batting, and backing; baste the layers together. Quilt as desired. I free-motion quilted meandering lines with flowers dispersed throughout.

2 Referring to "Binding" on page 75 and using the black-and-white 2½" strips, bind the edges of the quilt. Add a label if desired.

"Island Dreaming"

Pieced and quilted by Kate Henderson ● Finished quilt: 60½" x 60½" ● Finished block: 6" x 6"

Island Dreaming

Bright batiks will let you imagine you are on a tropical island, even in the middle of a very cold winter.

Materials

Yardage is based on 42"-wide fabric.

Fabric: *Poems from Pebbles by Malka Dubrawsky for Moda Fabrics*

40 strips, 2½" x 42", of assorted bright prints for blocks
3 yards of white fabric for background
⅝ yard of red print for binding
3⅞ yards of fabric for backing
69" x 69" piece of batting

Cutting

From *each of 20* bright strips, cut:
    3 rectangles, 2½" x 6½" (60 total)
    3 rectangles, 2½" x 4½" (60 total)
    3 squares, 2½" x 2½" (60 total)
From *each of 20* bright strips, cut:
    2 rectangles, 2½" x 6½" (40 total)
    2 rectangles, 2½" x 4½" (40 total)
    2 squares, 2½" x 2½" (40 total)
From the white fabric, cut:
    38 strips, 2½" x 42"; crosscut into:
        100 rectangles, 2½" x 4½"
        400 squares, 2½" x 2½"
From the red print, cut:
    7 strips, 2½" x 42"

Making the Blocks

For each block, use the same bright print in all steps. Press all seam allowances toward the print fabrics unless otherwise noted.

1 Referring to "Half-Square-Triangle Units" on page 72, make a half-square-triangle unit using one bright and one white 2½" square.

2 Referring to "Triangle Corners" on page 72, use a white 2½" square to make a triangle corner at one end of a bright 2½" x 4½" rectangle, matching the bright print from step 1.

 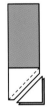

3 Use a white 2½" square to make a triangle corner at one end of a bright 2½" x 6½" rectangle, matching the bright print from steps 1 and 2.

4 Sew a white 2½" x 4½" rectangle to one end of the unit from step 1.

5 Sew a white 2½" square to one end of the unit from step 2.

6 Join the units from steps 4, 5, and 3 in order as shown to make a block. Press the seam allowances toward unit 3. Make 100 blocks.

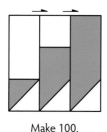

Make 100.

Quilt Assembly

Arrange the blocks in 10 rows of 10 blocks each, rotating the blocks as shown in the quilt assembly diagram. Sew the blocks together in rows. Press the seam allowances in opposite directions from row to row. Join the rows. Press the seam allowances in one direction.

Finishing the Quilt

1 Layer the quilt top, batting, and backing; baste the layers together. Quilt as desired. I free-motion quilted a pattern of overlapping triangles.

2 Referring to "Binding" on page 75 and using the red strips, bind the edges of the quilt. Add a label if desired.

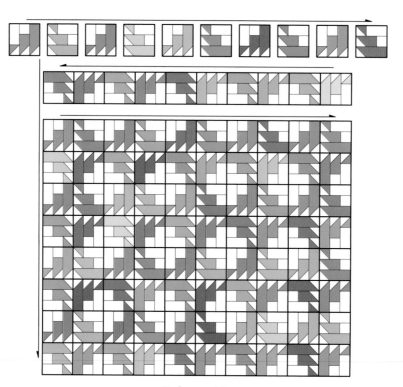

Quilt assembly

Barn Dance

Making a large quilt can seem like a big undertaking, but these big blocks go together quickly. Your quilt will be finished before you know it.

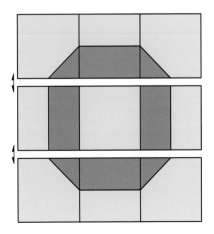

Materials

Yardage is based on 42"-wide fabric.

Fabric: *Various prints from my stash paired with Timeless Treasures Solids*

⅝ yard of a print for blocks and binding
½ yard *each* of 7 assorted prints for blocks and binding
1⅓ yards *each* of 4 assorted gray solids for backgrounds
7¾ yards of fabric for backing
93" x 93" piece of batting

Cutting

From the ⅝ yard of fabric, cut:
  7 strips, 2½" x 42"; crosscut *5 of the strips* into:
    16 squares, 2½" x 2½"
    8 rectangles, 2½" x 4½"
    8 rectangles, 2½" x 12½"

From *each* of the 7 assorted prints, cut:
  6 strips, 2½" x 42"; crosscut *5 of the strips* into:
    16 squares, 2½" x 2½" (112 total)
    8 rectangles, 2½" x 4½" (56 total)
    8 rectangles, 2½" x 12½" (56 total)

From *each* of the 4 gray solids, cut:
  5 strips, 4½" x 42"; crosscut into 36 squares,
    4½" x 4½" (144 total)
  8 strips, 2½" x 42"; crosscut into:
    16 rectangles, 2½" x 12½" (64 total)
    16 rectangles, 2½" x 4½" (64 total)

Making the Blocks

Press all seam allowances open.

1 Referring to "Triangle Corners" on page 72, make a triangle corner at one corner of a gray 4½" square with a print 2½" square. Make eight.

Make 8.

2 Using a matching print from step 1, sew together a gray and a print 2½" x 4½" rectangle along their long sides. Make four.

Make 4.

3 Sew units from step 2 to either side of a gray 4½" square.

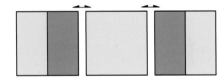

4 Sew units from step 1 to either side of a unit from step 2. Make two.

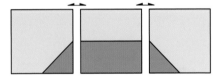

Make 2.

5 Sew the units from step 4 to the top and bottom of the unit from step 3.

"Barn Dance"

Pieced and quilted by Kate Henderson • **Finished quilt:** 80½" x 80½" • **Finished block:** 20" x 20"

6 Sew together a gray 2½" x 12½" rectangle and a matching print 2½" x 12½" rectangle along their long sides. Make four.

Make 4.

7 Sew units from step 6 to either side of the unit from step 5.

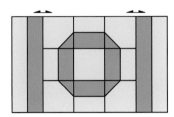

8 Sew a unit from step 1 to each end of a unit from step 6. Make two.

Make 2.

9 Sew the units from step 8 to the top and bottom of the unit from step 7. Repeat to make 16 blocks.

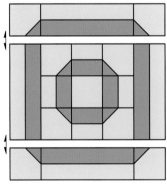

Make 16.

Quilt Assembly

Arrange the blocks in four rows of four blocks each. Sew the blocks together in rows, pressing the seam allowances open. Sew the rows together. Press the seam allowances open.

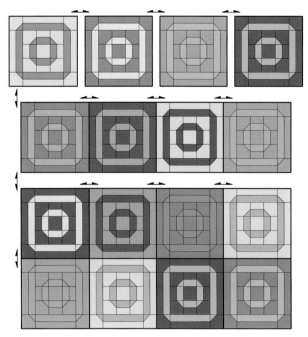

Quilt assembly

Finishing the Quilt

1 Layer the quilt top, batting, and backing; baste the layers together. Quilt as desired. I quilted straight vertical lines using a walking foot.

2 Referring to "Scrappy Binding" on page 75, join the print 2½" x 42" strips to make a long strip. Use the pieced strip to bind the edges of the quilt. Add a label if desired.

"Tulip Patch"

Pieced and quilted by Kate Henderson • Finished quilt: 60½" x 68½" • Finished block: 8" x 8"

Tulip Patch

Bright prints and tulips are two things that are guaranteed to make me smile. Make a tulip quilt, and you can always have a little bit of spring in your house throughout the year.

Materials

Yardage is based on 42"-wide fabric.

Fabric: *From my stash bucket*

25 strips, 2½" x 42", of assorted red, pink, yellow, and orange prints for blocks

25 strips, 2½" x 17", of assorted green prints for blocks

3⅝ yards of white fabric for blocks and border

⅝ yard of orange print for binding

3⅞ yards of fabric for backing

69" x 77" piece of batting

Cutting

From *each* of the 25 assorted red, pink, yellow, and orange strips, cut:

2 rectangles, 2½" x 8½" (50 total)

2 rectangles, 2½" x 4½" (50 total)

2 squares, 2½" x 2½" (50 total)

From *each* of the 25 green strips, cut:

1 rectangle, 2½" x 8½" (25 total)

2 rectangles, 2½" x 3½" (50 total)

From the white fabric, cut:

2 strips, 8½" x 42"; crosscut into 6 squares, 8½" x 8½"

5 strips, 4½" x 42"; crosscut into 50 rectangles, 4½" x 3½"

30 strips, 2½" x 42"; crosscut *23 of the strips* into:

25 rectangles, 2½" x 8½"

25 rectangles, 2½" x 4½"

50 rectangles, 2½" x 3½"

100 squares, 2½" x 2½"

2 strips, 1½" x 42"; crosscut into 50 squares, 1½" x 1½"

From the orange print, cut:

7 strips, 2½" x 42"

Making the Tulip Blocks

Press all seam allowances open.

1 Referring to "Triangle Corners" on page 72, use white 2½" squares to add a triangle corner to each end of a print 2½" x 8½" rectangle.

2 Use print 2½" squares that match the rectangle from step 1 to add a triangle corner to each end of a white 2½" x 8½" rectangle.

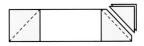

3 Place a print 2½" x 4½" rectangle that matches the print from steps 1 and 2 at right angles on a white 2½" x 4½" rectangle, right sides together. Draw a diagonal line from corner to corner across

the overlapped area. Stitch and trim as for "Triangle Corners." Repeat with a second print 2½" x 4½" rectangle on the other side. Be sure to orient the diagonal line as shown.

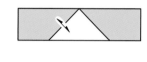

4 Arrange the units from steps 1, 2, and 3 with a matching print 2½" x 8½" rectangle as shown. Sew them together along their long edges. Make 25 tulip blocks.

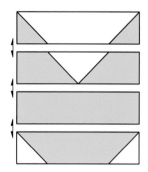

Make 25.

Making the Leaf and Stem Blocks

Press all seam allowances open.

1 Use white 2½" squares to add triangle corners to opposite corners of two matching green 2½" x 3½" rectangles.

2 Use white 1½" squares to add triangles to the corners opposite those you made in step 1.

3 Sew a white 2½" x 3½" rectangle to the top and a white 3½" x 4½" rectangle to the bottom of each unit from step 2.

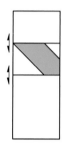

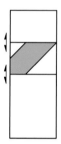

4 Sew the units from step 3 to each long side of a matching green 2½" x 8½" rectangle. Make 25 leaf and stem blocks.

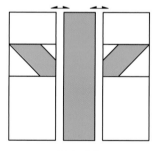

Make 25.

Quilt Assembly

1 Arrange the tulip blocks, leaf and stem blocks, and six white 8½" squares in eight rows of seven blocks each as shown in the quilt assembly diagram on page 61. Sew the blocks together into rows. Press the seam allowances open. Sew the rows together; press.

2 Sew the white 2½" x 42" strips together end to end. Press the seam allowances open. From the pieced strip, cut two side borders 64½" long and cut a top and a bottom border each 60½" long. Sew the 64½"-long border strips to the sides of the quilt. Press the seam allowances toward the borders. Sew the 60½"-long border strips to the top and the bottom of the quilt. Press the seam allowances toward the borders.

Finishing the Quilt

1 Layer the quilt top, batting, and backing; baste the layers together. Quilt as desired. I free-motion quilted a pattern of swirls and flowers.

2 Referring to "Binding" on page 75 and using the orange strips, bind the edges of the quilt. Add a label if desired.

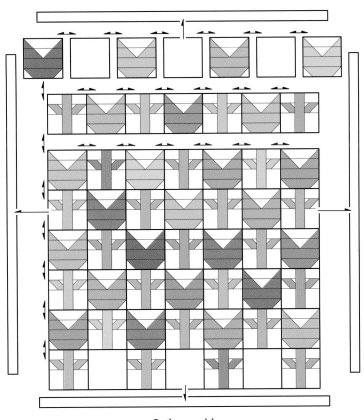

Quilt assembly

"Twinkle Twinkle"

Pieced and quilted by Kate Henderson • **Finished quilt: 61¼" x 64½"**

Twinkle Twinkle

Contrast is the key here. Lots of light prints in the background make the bright prints for the stars really shine. Or you might try this in reverse with white stars and a scrappy background.

Materials

Yardage is based on 42"-wide fabric.

Fabric: *From my stash bucket*

10 strips, 2½" x 42", of assorted bright prints for stars

64 strips, 2½" x 42", of assorted light prints for background

⅝ yard of blue print for binding

3⅞ yards of fabric for backing

70" x 73" piece of batting

60° triangle ruler or template plastic

Cutting

From the blue print, cut:

7 strips, 2½" x 42"

Making the Triangles

1 Organize the 10 bright 2½" x 42" strips into five pairs. Sew each pair of strips together along their long edges. Press the seam allowances open.

Make 5.

2 Referring to "Templates" on page 70, use the pattern on page 64 to make a 60° triangle template and align the blunted point with one long raw edge of the fabric. Align the base of the triangle with the opposite raw edge. Trace along the template's angled edges and cut. Rotate the template 180° and position it next to the angled cut edge, making sure the top and bottom of the triangle align with the fabric edges. Cut a second triangle. Repeat to cut a total of 12 triangles from each strip set (10 groups of six matching triangles—you'll only need nine groups).

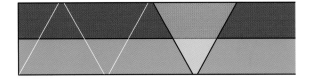

Ruler Instructions

To use a 60° triangle ruler, follow the manufacturer's instructions to cut triangles.

3 Organize the 64 light 2½" x 42" strips into pairs. Sew each pair of strips together along their long edges. Press the seam allowances open.

4 Cut each pair into 12 triangles as described in step 2 (384 triangles total; 6 will be left over).

Quilt Assembly

1 Arrange the triangles in 16 rows of 27 triangles. Use the quilt assembly diagram on page 64 to place the nine bright stars. It also shows how I arranged each light triangle, but they can be placed anywhere you like, so play around with them until you're happy with

the arrangement. Sew the triangles together into rows and press the seam allowances open. Sew the rows together; press the seam allowances open.

Quilt assembly

2 Trim the sides of the quilt ¼" past the edge of the triangles.

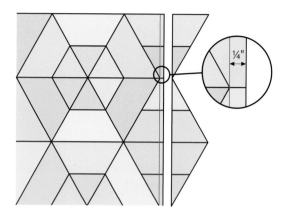

Finishing the Quilt

1 Layer the quilt top, batting, and backing; baste the layers together. Quilt as desired. I free-motion quilted pebbles over the backing triangles.

2 Referring to "Binding" on page 75 and using the blue-print strips, bind the edges of the quilt. Add a label if desired.

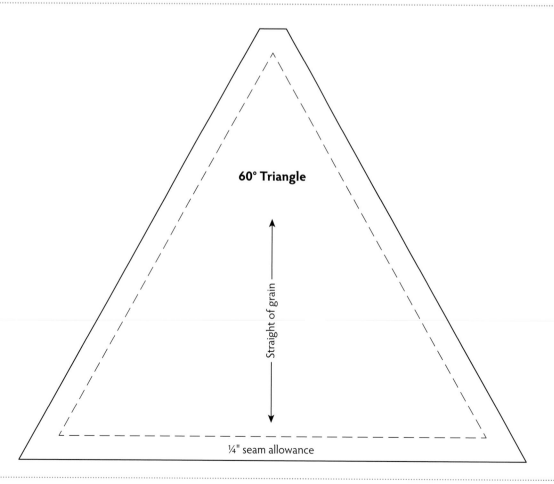

60° Triangle

Straight of grain

¼" seam allowance

Mosaic

*Each block in this quilt uses one print strip, so it's easy to make
it any size you want. Just add more strips and background!*

Materials

Yardage is based on 42"-wide fabric.

Fabric: *Color Theory by V & Co. for Moda Fabrics*

36 strips, 2½" x 42", of assorted prints for blocks and
    cornerstones

5 yards of white print for block background and
    sashing strips

⅔ yard of gray print for binding

5 yards of fabric for backing*

90" x 90" piece of batting

**Depending on the width of your fabric, you may need three
lengths for backing or 7½ yards total.*

Cutting

From *each* of the 36 assorted-print strips, cut:
    4 rectangles, 2½" x 4½" (144 total)
    5 squares, 2½" x 2½" (180 total)
    1 square, 1½" x 1½" (36 total; 11 will be left over)

From the white print, cut:
    45 strips, 2½" x 42"; crosscut into:
        288 rectangles, 2½" x 4½"
        144 squares, 2½" x 2½"
    34 strips, 1½" x 42"; crosscut into:
        60 rectangles, 1½" x 12½"
        72 rectangles, 1½" x 4½"
        72 rectangles, 1½" x 2½"

From the gray print, cut:
    8 strips, 2½" x 42"

Making the Blocks

1 Sew white 1½" x 2½" rectangles
to the top and bottom of a print
2½" square. Press the seam allowances
toward the square.

2 Sew a white 1½" x 4½" rectangle to each side of the
unit from step 1. Press the seam allowances toward
the center.

3 Sew together a print and a white 2½" x 4½"
rectangle along their long sides. Press the seam
allowances toward the print rectangle. Make four.

Make 4.

4 Sew together a print and a white 2½" square. Press
the seam allowances toward the print square.
Make four.

Make 4.

"Mosaic"

Pieced and quilted by Kate Henderson   •   Finished quilt: 77½" x 77½"   •   Finished block: 12" x 12"

5 Sew a white 2½" x 4½" rectangle to one side of a unit from step 4. Sew a white 2½" x 4½" rectangle to the opposite side of another unit from step 4. Press the seam allowances away from the rectangles. Make two of each.

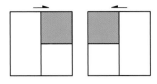

Make 2 of each.

6 Sew a unit from step 3 to each side of a unit from step 2 for the middle row. Press the seam allowances outward. Sew a unit from step 5 to each side of a unit from step 3. Press the seam allowances toward the middle. Make a second mirror-image row. Sew the rows together to make a block. Press the seam allowances outward. Make 36 blocks.

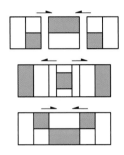
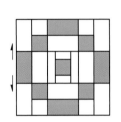

Make 36.

Quilt Assembly

1 Sew six of the white 1½" x 12½" rectangles and five of the print 1½" squares together as shown to make a sashing strip. Press the seam allowances toward the white rectangles. Make five sashing strips.

Make 5.

2 Sew six blocks and five white 1½" x 12½" rectangles together, alternating them as shown in the quilt assembly diagram. Press the seam allowances toward the white rectangles. Make six rows.

3 Lay out the assembled rows and sashing strips. Sew them together and press the seam allowances toward the sashing strips.

Finishing the Quilt

1 Layer the quilt top, batting, and backing; baste the layers together. Quilt as desired. I free-motion quilted swirls and loops.

2 Referring to "Binding" on page 75 and using the gray strips, bind the edges of the quilt. Add a label if desired.

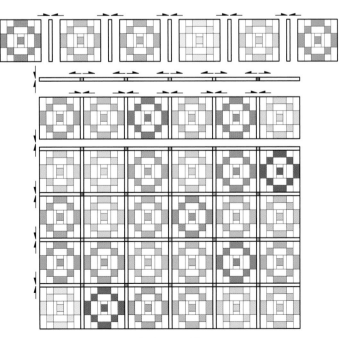

Quilt assembly

General Quiltmaking Instructions

This section contains all the information you'll need to complete your quilt. I've shared my preferred way of doing things and tips and techniques that I find useful.

Fabric

All the projects in this book are based on fabric with a 42" usable width. I used 100% cotton fabrics for all of the projects, but voile, flannel, linen, and corduroy are all good alternatives.

Collecting 2½"-Wide Strips

The easiest way to get 2½"-wide strips for your project is to buy them precut. Moda and many other fabric companies package precut 2½"-wide strips of their lines. Moda Jelly Rolls usually include 40 strips, which is perfect for a lot of projects in this book. Check the label to determine how many strips are included in a specific roll or bundle of strips.

There are lots of other ways to get 2½"-wide strips. When I buy a length of fabric, I always cut off a 2½"-wide strip and add it to my collection. If you like to buy fat quarters, cut two strips, 2½" wide, along the width of the fat quarter (21") and you will have the equivalent of one full-width strip. Each square in a Moda Layer Cake can be cut into four strips, 2½" x 10".

To use scraps in strip quilts, go through your scrap stash and cut small scraps into 2½" squares or 2½" x 4½" rectangles. Cut larger scraps into 2½"-wide strips. Organize and store the pieces so they're ready to go when you're ready to sew.

If you're not sure where to start with a scrappy quilt, or you're unsure about choosing a color theme, start with a few fabrics from the same fabric line, and then add other pieces with coordinating colors and shapes. Don't overthink; just grab what first catches your eye.

If a strip from your Jelly Roll is too similar to the background fabric, or a strip is standing out too much, replace it with another fabric from your stash, or buy a little extra binding or background fabric and cut an extra strip from that.

Fabric Preparation and Storage

Jelly Rolls should not be prewashed; putting one into the washing machine will just result in a tangled mess of fabric. I no longer prewash any of my fabric, and I haven't had any disasters when washing my quilts for the first time. I do add a dye catcher to the washing machine, especially if the quilt includes dark or red fabrics, as they sometimes run or bleed excess dye.

Jelly Rolls and fabric strips will often have a strong crease where they're folded in half. Unfold and press each strip so it's flat when cut, but take care not to distort the strip as you press.

There are many ways to store 2½"-wide strips. I like to store my 2½" squares and 2½" x 4½" rectangles in large clear cookie jars where I can see what's in there. I try to keep long strips in a tub all neatly folded up or wound, but I admit that, more often than I like, they end up all tangled, and I have to dig through to find what I want. Find a system that works for you; sort either by size or by color and use baskets or plastic tubs.

Rotary Cutting

You'll need to do some cutting even when a project begins with precuts, and rotary cutting is the easiest and most accurate method. Most of the projects in this book use basic square and rectangular rotary-cutting rulers. Having rulers of various sizes will simplify the cutting process, but you can manage with just a couple of lengths. I find it worth investing in a ruler and mat at least 24" long to make cutting strips from the width of the fabric very easy. To minimize waste, remember to cut the longest pieces from your strips first and the shortest pieces last.

Lefties

Reverse the following rotary-cutting instructions if you're left-handed.

1 If you're cutting your own strips from yardage, fold the fabric in half with the selvages aligned and place it on a cutting mat with the folded edge closest to you. Straighten one fabric edge by aligning a ruler line with the fold and cutting perpendicular to the fold. Turn the mat and fabric 180° to position them for cutting strips.

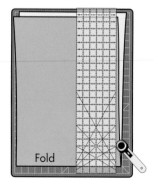

2 To cut a strip the desired width, align the ruler marking for that width with the trimmed edge of the fabric and cut along the right-hand edge of the ruler.

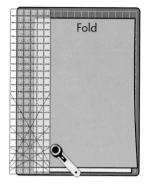

3 Trim the selvages from the ends of the strip, and it's ready for crosscutting into squares and rectangles.

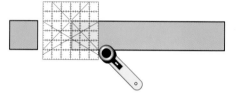

4 A couple of projects in this book require you to cut squares into triangles. Once you've cut the specified square, cut it in half diagonally from corner to corner for half-square triangles. Cut diagonally from all four corners for quarter-square triangles.

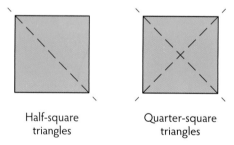

Half-square   Quarter-square
triangles   triangles

Templates

The only other rulers used for these projects are a 45° triangle for "Daydream" on page 21 and a 60° triangle for "Twinkle Twinkle" on page 63. Even these two rulers are optional; the pieces can be cut with a template. The pattern for the appropriate template can be found at the end of each project.

To make a template, trace the pattern for the template onto template plastic and cut it out. Lay the template on the assembled strip sets or strips as directed, mark the angle lines onto the fabric, and cut along the lines. Use scissors, or lay a ruler along the line and cut with a rotary cutter.

Seam Allowances

A ¼" seam allowance is used throughout this book. Even if you use a ¼" presser foot on your machine, it's worth checking to make sure you're sewing an accurate ¼"-wide seam allowance. A 60"-wide quilt made from 2½"-wide strips has many seams, and by the end you could be off by quite a bit!

To check your seam allowance, sew three 2½"-wide strips together and press. The finished unit should measure 6½" wide. If it measures more than 6½", increase the seam allowances by a thread's width (0.5 mm) or two. If it measures less than 6½", make the seam allowances correspondingly narrower. Keep testing until your seam allowance is exactly ¼" wide.

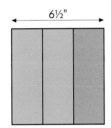

6½"

Thread

I use 100% cotton thread for all my piecing and machine quilting. I love Aurifil 50 weight and find it's perfect for piecing and quilting.

Pressing

Seam allowances can be pressed to one side or open. My only rule for pressing seam allowances is to do what you prefer. I tend to do a bit of both, and throughout this book, I indicate the pressing direction I used for each seam allowance.

I press seam allowances open in most of my blocks, especially when there are triangle or half-square corners. I think it makes for a flatter quilt top and a more precise matching of seams. If there's sashing in the quilt, I press the seam allowances to one side, usually toward the sashing. In quilts with mainly straight lines or simple quilts I want to make quickly, I press the seam allowances to one side.

Quick Piecing Techniques

After you've cut the pieces, its time to sew them together. Here are two techniques to make your piecing faster and more accurate.

Strip Piecing

Strip piecing is a great way to save time when you're making identical units out of 2½"-wide strips. To strip piece, sew the strips together along the long edges, and then crosscut the strip sets into units of the required shape and size. Cutting the units after you have sewn the strips together can be more accurate than piecing individual 2½" squares.

Chain Piecing

Chain piecing saves time and thread. Instead of sewing just two pieces of fabric together at a time, get a whole pile ready to sew. After you've sewn the first pair, leave the presser foot down, feed the next pair under the foot, and keep sewing. When all the pieces in the pile are sewn, lift the presser foot, cut the thread, and then cut the chains of thread between each pair.

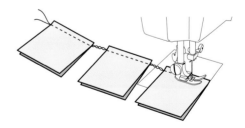

Special Piecing Techniques

Triangle corners (sometimes called folded corners), half-square-triangle units, and flying-geese units are used in many of the projects in this book. Here are some special sewing techniques that can speed up the process of making many of these units.

Triangle Corners

1 With a sharp pencil, draw a diagonal line from corner to corner across the wrong side of a 2½" square. Place the square at one end of a 2½"-wide strip, right sides together, and sew one thread width away from the drawn line on the seam-allowance side.

2 Fold the resulting triangle over the seamline to check that it matches the edges of the 2½"-wide strip, and adjust the stitching line if necessary. Return the square to the sewing position and trim the corner, leaving a ¼"-wide seam allowance. Fold the resulting triangle outward and press the seam allowances in the direction the project indicates.

To save time drawing lines on the many 2½" squares required for some of the projects, place a strip of masking tape on the sewing-machine bed as a guide for positioning the squares. Start sewing at the outer corner and align the square's opposite corner with the edge of the masking tape.

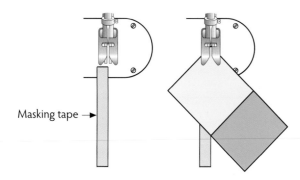

Masking tape →

Half-Square-Triangle Units

To make half-square-triangle units from two 2½" squares, follow the instructions for triangle corners using a second 2½" square in place of the 2½"-wide strip.

Flying-Geese Units

1 Each flying-geese unit uses two 2½" squares and a 2½" x 4½" rectangle. Draw diagonal lines from corner to corner across the wrong sides of both squares.

2 Place a square on one end of the rectangle, right sides together, and sew one thread width away from the drawn line on the seam-allowance side.

3 Fold the triangle over the seamline to check that it matches the edges of the rectangle and adjust the stitching line if necessary. Return the square to the sewing position and trim the corner, leaving a ¼"-wide seam allowance. Fold the resulting triangle outward and press the seam allowances open.

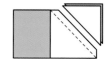

4 Repeat steps 2 and 3 to add the second square to the other end of the rectangle. Be sure to orient the seamlines to form a large triangle in the middle of the unit.

 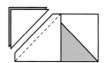

Sashing and Borders

Within this book, the exact measurements for sashing and borders are given in each project's instructions, but it's a good idea to measure the quilt before attaching the borders to ensure that the quilt lies flat and straight. Measure the length of the pieced quilt top from raw edge to raw edge in two different places and average the measurements. Cut the side borders this length. Mark the centers of the quilt top and borders. Sew the borders in place, matching the center point and both ends. Press the seam allowances as indicated in the project instructions.

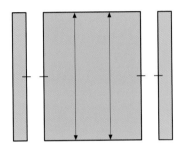

Measure the length in two places; match the centers.

Measure the width of the quilt top, including the side borders, in the same way. Cut and attach the borders as before. Press the seam allowances as indicated in the project instructions.

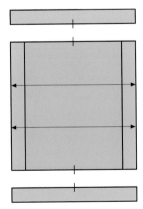

Include the borders in the width measurement.

Quilt Sizes

Most of the quilts in this book can be made smaller or larger by eliminating or adding rows. To make a bigger quilt, grab more strips and keep sewing blocks until you have the quilt size you want. Increase the sizes of the batting and backing pieces to accommodate the new pieces.

Quilting the Quilt

When the piecing is complete, you'll need to add backing and batting for loft and to finish the back of the quilt.

Backing

The backing measurements in each project allow at least 3" beyond the quilt top on all sides. For most of the quilts in the book you'll have to piece the backing.

Remove the selvages from the fabric and cut the purchased piece in half across the width. Align the lengthwise edges of the two pieces, right sides together, and sew using a ½"-wide seam allowance. Press the seam allowances open.

Which Way?

The backing seam can run either horizontally or vertically across the quilt. The instructions give the minimum possible yardage for the backing, which may mean that its lengthwise grain runs across the width of the quilt. If you prefer a vertical seam, recalculate the yardage and purchase more fabric if necessary.

To make a more interesting backing, you can incorporate leftover strips from the quilt top or make extra blocks to stitch the backing. Use your imagination and make the backing as interesting as the front.

Batting

I use 100% cotton batting in my quilts. I machine quilt them all on a domestic machine and find cotton batting easy to manage. I also like the low-loft look of cotton batting and live in a climate where warm quilts aren't needed. Cotton batting is easy to machine wash and dry, which is important in my house; we use the quilts all the time, and my children play on and build playhouses with them.

Different types of batting create slightly different looks when quilted, so experiment with several and use the one you prefer.

Basting

To baste the quilt, spread the backing wrong side up on a flat surface, such as a table (or two placed side by side) or the floor. I have a wooden floor and always baste my quilts there. Smooth the backing until it's flat and secure the edges to the floor or table with masking tape. Center the batting over the backing, smoothing out any wrinkles. Center the quilt top over the batting right side up and smooth into place.

If you'll be machine quilting, baste the layers together by placing safety pins every 3" to 4" through all the layers. I find it best to start in the middle and work toward the edges. Other basting methods include long hand-basting stitches and basting sprays. Choose the one that works best for your quilting preferences.

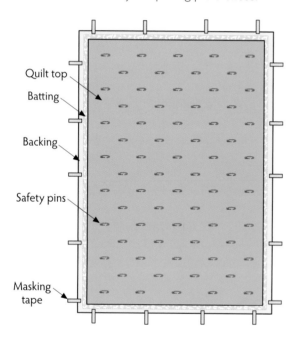

Quilt top
Batting
Backing
Safety pins
Masking tape

Quilting

I like to machine quilt all my own quilts on a domestic sewing machine. There is something magical about seeing a quilt top transform into a quilt, and I'm always so impatient to see a quilt finished. I don't have to wait if I do the quilting myself. You can quilt in straight lines using a walking foot, employ free-motion techniques, or use a combination of both. I've included a description of my quilting at the end of each project.

If you're new to machine quilting, a good place to start is sewing straight lines that follow the lines of the quilt. I like to use the edge of my walking foot as a guide to stitch along both sides of a seam, positioning the quilting lines about 1" apart. Test different stitch lengths

on your machine when using a walking foot; I find my quilting stitches look best when they're slightly longer than my piecing stitches.

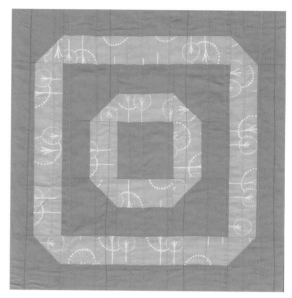

Straight vertical lines quilted with a walking foot

Simple meandering lines make a good introduction to free-motion quilting. Lower or cover the feed dogs and use a darning foot or one specifically meant for free-motion quilting. Make a mini quilt from fabric and batting scraps to practice on before working on a big quilt; free-motion quilting becomes easier with practice. When you're satisfied with your meandering, try adding loops and flowers as you quilt.

Overlapping triangles

Free-motion loop design

Allover wave pattern

Binding

I make different types of bindings, either from a variety of scraps or from a single fabric. A binding can frame a quilt and provide contrast to the quilt design, it can complement the design and fabrics in the quilt, or it can blend in with the background. Often I don't choose the binding fabric until I've finished the top so that I can audition several fabrics and see which one I prefer. For all my bindings, I cut strips across the fabric width rather than on the bias. I machine stitch the binding from the front of the quilt, fold it over the raw edges, and hand sew it to the backing.

Scrappy Binding

The great thing about making quilts with 2½"-wide strips is that those strips are also the perfect width for binding; it's so easy to collect the scraps of strips and sew them together for the binding. I sew the scraps together end to end to minimize waste, and I prefer this look to diagonal seams when I'm using scraps.

Use ½"-wide seam allowances and press them open to minimize bulk. Before attaching the binding to the quilt, make sure none of the seams end up on the quilt corners, where the extra bulk can make sewing the binding difficult.

Scrappy binding using the same fabrics as in the quilt top adds interest.

One-Fabric Binding

Remove the selvages from the binding strips and sew the strips together with diagonal seams as shown. Trim the excess fabric, leaving a ¼"-wide seam allowance, and press the seam allowances open.

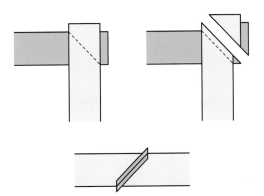

Press seam allowances open.

Attaching the Binding

1. Fold the binding strip in half lengthwise, wrong sides together, and press.

2. Trim the excess batting and backing to match the quilt top. Using a walking foot and a ¼" seam allowance, start sewing the binding to the quilt, leaving about 10" of binding unstitched at the start. Stop sewing ¼" before the corner, and backstitch.

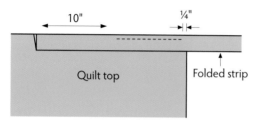

3. Position the quilt for sewing the second side. Fold the binding up and then back down on itself, aligning the raw edges with the second side of the quilt. Stitch the binding to the second side of the quilt using a ¼" seam allowance, stopping and backstitching ¼" before the next corner. Repeat around the quilt. Finish sewing 5" to 6" from the beginning of the stitching and take the quilt out of the machine.

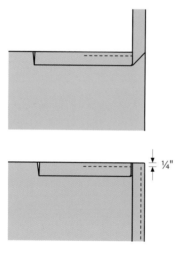

4. To join a one-fabric binding, lay the ends of the binding strip on top of each other and trim, leaving a 2½" overlap. Unfold the binding ends and position them right sides together and at right angles, as you did when sewing the binding strips. Pin the pieces in place and sew from corner to corner. Trim the excess fabric, leaving a ¼"-wide seam allowance.

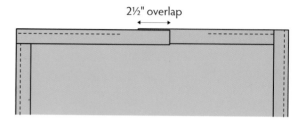

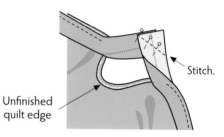

5. If you're using scrappy binding, lay the binding ends on top of each other and trim, leaving a ½" overlap. Unfold the ends of the binding and, with right sides together, sew the ends using a ¼"-wide seam allowance.

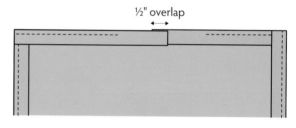

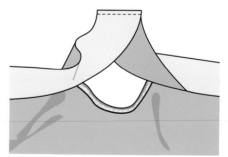

Stitch ends together.

6 For either method, finger-press the seam allowances open, refold the binding, and finish sewing it to the quilt. Fold the binding to the back of the quilt, covering the raw edges, and hand stitch it in place, mitering the corners.

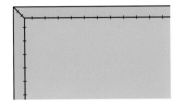

Quilt back

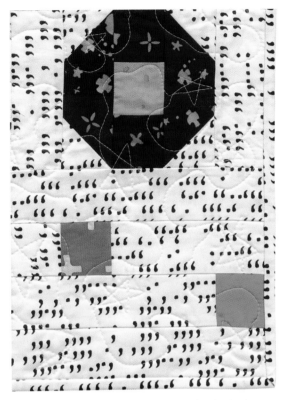

Matching binding gives a cohesive look.

Contrasting binding frames the quilt.

Acknowledgments

Thanks to my husband, Chris, and my girls, Grace, Amelia, Eva, and Olive, for believing in me and for all your help with choosing fabrics and for loving the quilts I make for you.

Thank you to the following fabric manufacturers for providing me with beautiful fabric: Moda, Timeless Treasures, Andover, and Ella Blue. Thank you to Aurifil for the wonderful thread.

Thank you to everyone at Martingale for your encouragement, support, and professionalism.

Thanks to everyone in the online quilting and crafting community. When I started a craft blog 10 years ago, I had no idea I would meet so many amazingly creative, interesting, and supportive people.

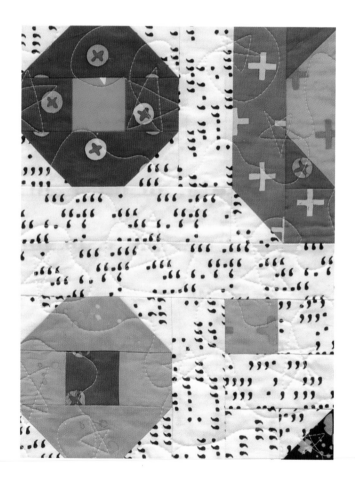

Meet Kate Henderson

Kate learned to sew clothes at the age of 12 and has sewn for herself ever since. After her twins were born in 2005, she began designing soft toys for them and to sell as a way to keep sane while her babies were little. Soon she began selling patterns for the toys and for the quilts she was making.

Kate's first book was *Strip Savvy* (Martingale, 2014). Her work has also appeared in *Modern Quilts from the Blogging Universe* (Martingale, 2012) and in *That Patchwork Place® Quilt Calendar 2015*.

She lives in the southwest of Western Australia with her husband and four girls, and she blogs at twolittlebanshees.com about her crafting adventures and her life.

More books to love!

Find these books at your friendly neighborhood quilt shop
or at ShopMartingale.com.

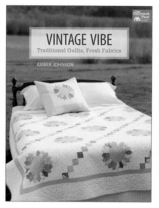

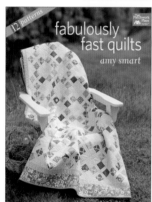

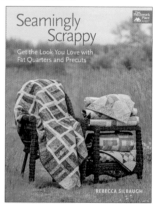

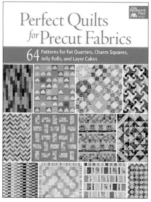

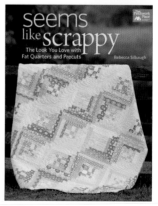